# THE TABLETOP LEARNING SERIES

# PUPPETS

## Friends at Your Finger Tips
by Imogene Forte

Incentive Publications, Inc.
Nashville, Tennessee

*Illustrated by Susan Eaddy*
*Cover designed by Mary Hamilton and illustrated by Jan Cunningham*
*Edited by Susan Oglander*

Library of Congress Catalog Number 84-62934
ISBN 0-86530-101-8

THE TABLETOP LEARNING SERIES™ is a trademark of Incentive Publications, Inc., Nashville, TN 37215

# THIS
# PUPPET BOOK
# BELONGS TO

Brenda M. Decker

# CONTENTS

ix     A Note to Kids

**PUPPETS**

12     Finger Frolics
14     Shadow, Shadow on the Wall
16     Rock 'n Roland
17     Winifred Walrus
18     Garden Party
20     Leaping Lizards
21     Cutouts To Cut Up
22     Santa and His Elves
24     Let Your Fingers Do the Walking
25     Shape Up
26     Heads Up
29     Bathtub Benny
30     Clothespin Cowboys
31     Spongy Spaceman
32     Harry Hairbrush
33     Sweep Him off His Feet
34     Pancake Turner Tom and Friend
35     Cereal Box Cecilia
36     Slithery Snake
38     Sam Spud, Sarah Spud
39     Wally the Walnut
40     Puppets on a Picnic
42     Monsters on the Prowl
44     Balloon Bogeymen

45    "Wooden" You Like a Puppet?
46    Pop-up Puppets
47    Gypsy Rose Rises Again
48    A Royal Court
50    Marionette Magic
52    A Mitten or a Kitten?
53    Thumb Along
54    Fancy Flora and Faded Fred
56    Isn't It Amazing What a Hand Can Do?
58    Ten Little Glove Fingers
59    Feet First
60    Rabbit Rally
62    An Old Sweater Never Had It Better
63    See You Later, Alligator

## MORE ABOUT PUPPETS

66    Materials To Collect and Save for Puppet Making
68    Put Your Puppets on Stage
70    Tips for Writing Puppet Plays
73    And They Lived Happily Ever After
74    Fairy Tales for Puppets To Act Out
76    One Person Does the Talking

78    INDEX

# A NOTE TO KIDS

## *Ten reasons why making the puppets in this book will be fun for you to do!*

1. They are quick and easy to make. Most of them can be completed in less than an hour.
2. Your "puppet maker's" kit can be put together almost entirely with things you would ordinarily have on hand around the house or in the classroom.
3. You won't need a lot of space to work. In fact, your puppet maker's kit will be just perfect to take in a car, train, boat or plane.
4. All the directions for making the puppets are simple, easy to follow, and each one has been planned to let you add your own "creative touch."
5. You can make one puppet at a time to add to a "made-by-you" collection. Before you know it, you will have a puppet collection that you will really be proud to show off.
6. Each puppet in the collection can be used by itself or with other puppets (and other people) in group activities.
7. Suggestions for props and plays are included to get your puppetry well under way.
8. You can make puppets for special, inexpensive gifts. For example, Santa and His Elves would add a happy note to any Christmas celebration.
9. You can also use your creations as place cards, decorations, visual aids for book reports or other presentations and as package tie-ons.
10. Making the puppets in this book will serve as a springboard to help you think and behave more creatively. Before you know it, you will be making up puppet characters of your own to add to the ones in this book.

Imogene Forte

# PUPPETS

# FINGER FROLICS

*for a fanciful play*

## WHAT TO USE:
- tape
- tracing paper
- white paper
- scissors
- felt tip pens
- cellophane tape
- pencil

## WHAT TO DO:
1. Trace the finger puppets on the next page onto the white paper.
2. Color the puppets with felt tip pens and cut them out.
3. Tape them together as shown in the diagram.
4. Make up a play and ask two friends to help you present it. Or, just make up the play as you go along, allowing each person to make up the part for his or her puppet.

With leaping leprechauns, a lovely lassie and a lonely lad you will have lots of possibilities for an action-packed play.

# SHADOW, SHADOW ON THE WALL

*some fat, some skinny, some tall, tall, tall*

**WHAT TO USE:**
- heavy colored paper
- cookie cutters
  (star, heart, boy or girl)
- straws
- tape
- scissors
- flashlight

14

## WHAT TO DO:

1. Use the cookie cutters as patterns to cut out characters for your play or objects for props. Cut them out of colored paper.
2. Tape the shapes to the straws.
3. Shine a flashlight on the puppets so they will cast shadows on the wall.

If you have the boy cookie cutter, you might want to use it to tell the story of the "Gingerbread Man."

# ROCK 'N ROLAND

*a masterful musician*

**WHAT TO USE:**
- cardboard roll from bathroom tissue
- construction paper
- scissors
- paper towel strips
- felt tip pens
- glue

**WHAT TO DO:**
1. Cut the cardboard roll long enough to fit two fingers.
2. Cut a piece of construction paper to fit around the roll and glue it in place.
3. Make sunglasses from black construction paper and glue those on.
4. Make some wild hair from strips of paper towels and color them bright yellow. Glue them to the top of the roll.
5. Make Roland a scarf and glue it around the bottom of the roll. Then, what else — rock and roll!!

# WINIFRED WALRUS

*she'll win your heart*

**WHAT TO USE:**
- brown paper bag
- construction paper
- glue
- felt tip pens
- scissors

**WHAT TO DO:**
1. Fold the paper bag flat against one side to make a space for your hand.
2. Give Winifred tusks, arms and a pretty hat.

Making Winifred (and/or her brother or sister) will get you off to a good start as a paper bag puppeteer. Collect your bags and make people, animals and critters of your own design.

# GARDEN PARTY

*when the flowers talk, everyone listens*

A

**WHAT TO USE:**
- 2 white paper plates
- glue
- paint or crayons
- scissors
- real leaves and stems

B

C

## WHAT TO DO:

1. Design the back of one paper plate with a pretty flower face.
2. Cut another plate in half and glue it to the face plate so the insides are facing each other. Your hand will fit in here to operate your puppet (see illustration).
3. Glue on real leaves and stems or use paint and crayons to give your flower personality. You can cut a hole for the mouth and stick your fingers out to make the flower talk.

You can make your play into a garden party and discuss all the things that flowers, plants, bugs and squirrels talk about when humans aren't around.

# LEAPING LIZARDS

*from construction paper*

**WHAT TO USE:**
- different colored construction paper
- scissors
- felt tip pens
- glue

**WHAT TO DO:**
1. Fold one piece of construction paper into thirds lengthwise.
2. Then, fold the paper in half.
3. Stick your fingers in the top half and your thumb in the bottom half to open and close the puppet's mouth.
4. Use the other colors of construction paper to decorate the lizard with scales, eyes, nose and long tongue. Glue all these features on.

You can make some other animals to add to a "reptile" zoo — try a snake, crocodile or a turtle.

A      B      C

# CUTOUTS TO CUT UP

*for finger puppets*

## WHAT TO USE:
- old catalogs and/or magazines
- sturdy white paper
- glue
- tape
- scissors

## WHAT TO DO:
1. Look through the magazines or catalogs for pictures of people or animals to use as finger puppet characters. (Remember, look for pictures that will "fit your fingers.")
2. Cut out the pictures.
3. Glue them onto paper strips to make puppets (see diagram).
4. Make up a play for your puppets.

As a matter of fact, you just may want to use these puppets as characters for your own soap opera — you could write new episodes to take them through all sorts of interesting situations.

# SANTA AND HIS ELVES

*your fingers will bring them to life!*

**WHAT TO USE:**
- white paper
- tape
- construction paper
- felt tip pens
- yarn, cotton
- other odds and ends
- scissors

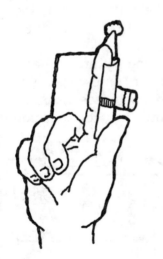

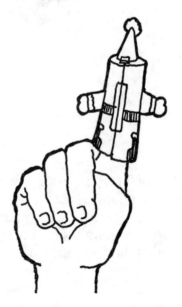

**WHAT TO DO:**
1. Cut a strip of paper to fit around your finger. Use this as a pattern to cut out additional strips.
2. Use the felt tip pens, construction paper, yarn and other odds and ends to make Santa and his elves.
3. Wrap the paper around your finger to make a tube.
4. When the tube is fully decorated, use tape to fasten it together.

You might want to make some reindeer too!

# LET YOUR FINGERS DO THE WALKING

*and your mouth do the talking*

**WHAT TO USE:**
- white paper
- pencil
- felt tip pens
- scissors
- posterboard
- glue

**WHAT TO DO:**
1. Draw characters on the white paper, making them approximately 5" tall.
2. Be sure to draw two circles for your fingers.
3. Color the characters with felt tip pens.
4. Cut the characters out.
5. Cut a piece of posterboard the same shape and size as the character.
6. Glue the character to the posterboard.
7. Carefully cut out the holes for your fingers in each puppet. (Ask for help if you need it.)
8. Stick your fingers through the holes to make the legs for your character, then let your fingers do the walking!

# SHAPE UP

*or ship out*

## WHAT TO USE:

- shirt cardboard or heavy white paper
- pencil
- felt tip pens (different colors)
- sticks
- glue
- scissors
- strips of construction paper

## WHAT TO DO:

1. Draw different kinds of shapes on the cardboard or paper.
2. Use the felt tip pens to give each shape a personality of its own.
3. Cut out the shapes and glue on the sticks.
4. Use folded or fringed paper strips to make arms and legs.
5. Use your puppets to present the most imaginative ship-shape play you can think of. You could use monsters, magicians, men from Mars or . . . .

# PAPIER MÂCHÉ

## *for any old day*

This is a messy job. Be sure to ask the grownups for advice about a work spot. Then, cover your entire work area with an old plastic tablecloth, shower curtain or layers and layers of newspaper. Remember too, this project takes a while to do so it isn't one you can clean up after right away.

**WHAT TO USE:**
- large plastic container
- lots of newspaper
- water
- paste
- vegetable grater (if you have one)
- old fork
- stick or wooden spoon

## WHAT TO DO:

1. Tear newspaper into strips.
2. Fill a plastic dishpan, wastebasket or bucket with hot water.
3. Crumple up the newspaper strips and put them in the hot water.
4. Use a stick or an old wooden spoon to stir the newspaper strips around in the water so that they are all covered.
5. Leave the paper to soak for a good while (overnight if you have the time).
6. Take the soaked paper out of the bucket, a handful at a time, and squeeze out as much of the water as you can.
7. Break up all the "clumps." Use a vegetable or cheese grater to make this process easier if you have one. If not, just keep working at it by pulling and kneading.
8. After you have the paper as fine and as dry as possible, empty all the water in the bucket and put the pulp back in the bucket.
9. Then, use an old fork to stir in enough paste to make the pulp a good working consistency (it should feel about as firm as play dough or clay). You may need to use your hands to mix too.
10. Form the well-mixed papier mâché into a big ball and store it in a plastic container until you are ready to begin making your puppet head.

27

# HEADS UP

*add a face, and you're in business*

Once you learn to look for all kinds of things to use for puppet heads, you are well on your way to becoming a creative puppeteer.

Once you have selected the type of head you want to use, determining the type of puppet to make will be easy. You can use the same head to make a rod or stick puppet, a hand puppet or a marionette. Some things you might want to begin your collection with . . .

- balls of all kinds (tennis, pingpong, softball)
- balloons
- blown-out egg shells
- modeling clay
- homemade play dough
- newspaper stripping

You will find a recipe for making papier mâché puppet heads on page 26.

# BATHTUB BENNY

*a friend in the tub is a friend indeed*

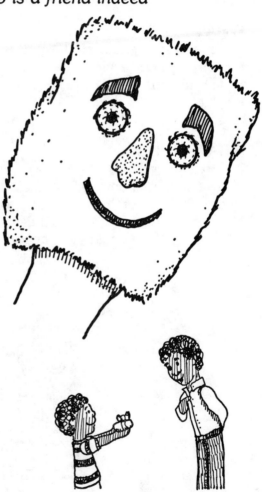

**WHAT TO USE:**
- washcloth or old hand towel
- needle and thread
- felt

**WHAT TO DO:**
1. Sew up the sides of a washcloth or hand towel, leaving a space for your hand.
2. Cut out facial features from felt and sew them in place.

You can insert a bar of soap and give it to someone special as a gift!

# CLOTHESPIN COWBOYS

*these guys will spring into action*

**WHAT TO USE:**
- several spring-type clothespins
- construction paper
- felt tip pens
- glue
- scissors

**WHAT TO DO:**
1. Decide what type of cowboys you want to make.
2. Use construction paper and felt tip pens to make boots, a hat, a checkered shirt, spurs or anything else you can imagine.
3. Glue the items on the clothespins and use the springs to make them operate. (You could even decorate one as a horse!)

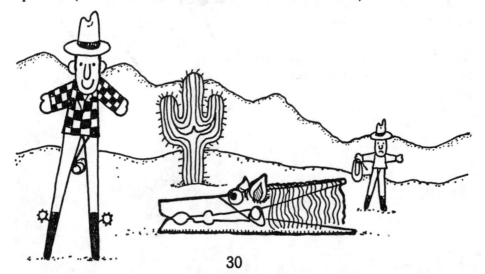

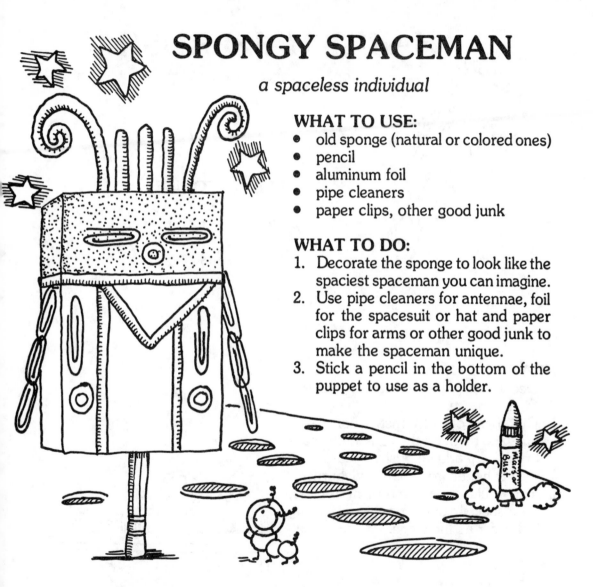

# SPONGY SPACEMAN

*a spaceless individual*

**WHAT TO USE:**
- old sponge (natural or colored ones)
- pencil
- aluminum foil
- pipe cleaners
- paper clips, other good junk

**WHAT TO DO:**
1. Decorate the sponge to look like the spaciest spaceman you can imagine.
2. Use pipe cleaners for antennae, foil for the spacesuit or hat and paper clips for arms or other good junk to make the spaceman unique.
3. Stick a pencil in the bottom of the puppet to use as a holder.

31

# HARRY HAIRBRUSH

*his name says it all*

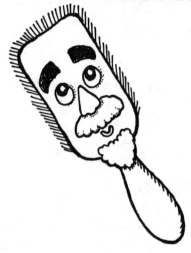

**WHAT TO USE:**
- old hairbrush
- construction paper
- glue
- scissors

**WHAT TO DO:**
1. Decide what kind of features you want to give Harry.
2. Cut them out of construction paper and glue them on the back of the hairbrush. Try adding bushy eyebrows, a mustache, beard or long sideburns.
3. You could use a comb or mirror too, for a special puppet play, maybe using a dresser as the stage.

# SWEEP HIM OFF HIS FEET

*with a broom puppet*

**WHAT TO USE:**
- broom
- old solid-colored pillowcase
- yarn
- paints and paintbrush
- glue

**WHAT TO DO:**
1. Cover the bristle side of the broom with the pillowcase.
2. Tie it in place with a piece of yarn.
3. Gather lots of yarn together and glue in place for hair.
4. Paint a beautiful face on the pillowcase and get ready to take that sweep at him!

These make great life-size puppets to dance with or talk to or to stand in the corner of your room.

May I have this dance?

# PANCAKE TURNER TOM AND FRIEND

*flip it for a new face*

**WHAT TO USE:**
- plastic pancake turner
- noodles, rice, nuts
- paper towel strips
- felt tip pens
- glue

**WHAT TO DO:**
1. Find an old pancake turner that you can bring to life!
2. On one side, glue on noodle eyes, a nut nose and a rice mouth.
3. Color the paper towel strips with the felt tip pens and glue them on for hair.
4. On the other side, make another face varying the ingredients for the facial features. (The hair will work either way you flip it!)

# CEREAL BOX CECILIA

*what a boxy personality!*

## WHAT TO USE:
- empty individual-sized cereal box
- scissors or sharp knife
- felt
- glue
- yarn
- buttons
- felt tip pens

## WHAT TO DO:
1. Cut three sides of the cereal box and bend the sides back to fit your hand.
2. Cover the box with felt and glue in place.
3. Give Cecilia black or yellow yarn hair, buttons for eyes and draw on a pair of rosy red lips. Talk about personality!!

# SLITHERY SNAKE

*you never knew what a sock could do*

**WHAT TO USE:**
- old argyle or striped sock
- needle and thread
- buttons
- other odds and ends

**WHAT TO DO:**
1. Place your hand in the toe of the sock so that the elastic part reaches your forearm. The toe end will be the snake's face.
2. Sew on the buttons for eyes.
3. Add other trim and odds and ends to make your snake more interesting.

An argyle sock will look like a diamondback rattle-snake and the striped one like a coral snake. See if you can find out more about snakes and how they slither!

# SAM SPUD, SARAH SPUD

*and lots of little spuds*

**WHAT TO USE:**
- potatoes
- glue
- toothpicks
- seeds, nuts, noodles
- pipe cleaners
- construction paper scraps

**WHAT TO DO:**
1. Decorate the potatoes to resemble Sam and Sarah. (You could use the big, brown potatoes for them and smaller red ones for the "little spuds.")
2. Use seeds, nuts, pipe cleaners and other items to give your potato characters personalities of their own. (You could use other vegetables too.)

# WALLY
# THE WALNUT

*and his nutty trio*

**WHAT TO USE:**
- walnut shell halves
- sticks
- rice, pasta, other nuts
- glue

**WHAT TO DO:**
1. Glue rice and other kitchen items onto the walnut shell to make a face.
2. Glue the walnut shell to the end of the stick.
3. Make a few more nutty puppets for a nutty marathon race, wedding or jumping contest. (Don't forget to eat the insides for a nutty treat!)

# PUPPETS ON A PICNIC

*almost as much fun as lunch*

**WHAT TO USE:**

- plastic spoons, knives and forks
- paper or Styrofoam plates, bowls and cups
- paper napkins
- rubber bands
- homemade paste
- pebbles, leaves, twigs
- other odds and ends

## WHAT TO DO:

1. After the picnic lunch (or lunch at school), gather up any leftover picnic supplies that look like they could be used for puppet making. The only thing you will have to plan ahead for is to take a tiny jar of paste. Just remember to tuck it in your pocket or the basket before leaving home. Of course, if you really want to get fancy, you could smuggle in a few other goodies like crayons, fabric, yarn scraps and so on. But, you can make perfectly fine puppets without the extras. Actually, it is almost more fun to use just the leftovers because it makes you use your imagination more.

2. Talk with your friends about the kind of puppet play you want to present. Decide on a plot and the characters. Then, let each person make the character he or she is to play.

3. It will be fun to see what kind of materials each puppet maker uses. You will most likely see some very creative puppets and an even more creative play.

# MONSTERS ON THE PROWL

*you will want to make 3 or 4
— maybe more*

**WHAT TO USE:**
- small frozen juice can
  (preferably paper)
- glue
- brown paper bag
- scissors
- kitchen twine (optional)
- beans, rice, pasta, dry cereal
- stick

**WHAT TO DO:**
1. Remove one end of the can and wash and dry it thoroughly.
2. Cut out a piece of the brown paper bag to cover the can.
3. Glue the paper on, making sure it completely covers one opening, and just tuck the ends into the other opening.

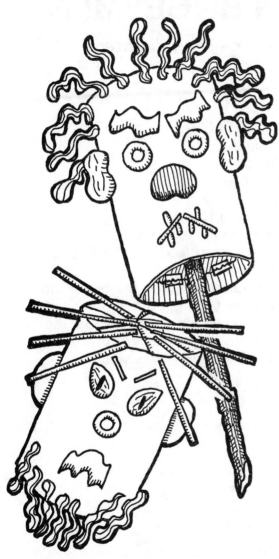

4. Select beans, rice, pasta, dry cereal or whatever's in the pantry to make the scariest face you can think of.
5. Shred strips of the paper bag or use kitchen twine to make hair and/or a beard.
6. Glue the stick to the inside of the can.

One puppet monster will be fun, but a pair of monsters will be more fun. Who knows, it may be like eating peanuts — once you have made one, you will want lots more!

# BALLOON BOGEYMEN

*just let out the air — they disappear*

## WHAT TO USE:
- balloons
- felt tip pens
- string

## WHAT TO DO:
1. Blow up the balloons.
2. Color scary faces on the balloons with felt tip pens.
3. Tie a string around the bottom to operate your puppet. If you want, you can let out the air and put the balloons on your fingers for a different kind of balloon puppet.

# "WOODEN" YOU LIKE A PUPPET?

*from a wooden scrap*

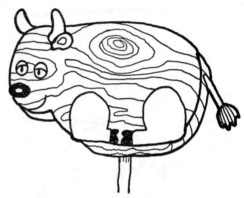

## WHAT TO USE:
- scraps of wood (different shapes and sizes)
- glue
- tissue, crepe or cellophane paper scraps
- scissors

## WHAT TO DO:
1. Search through the wood scraps until you find a shape that interests you. (This is especially fun if you know someone who has a woodworking shop and will save a big box of scraps for you.)
2. Look at the shape from all sides to see what character it suggests.
3. Then, cut facial features, hair and decorative trim (such as hat, tie, jacket, etc.) from the paper scraps and glue them in place.

If you are doing this alone, you might want to make characters for an entire play and save them until you have someone else to join you in acting out the play.

# POP-UP PUPPETS

*to pep up a dull day*

## WHAT TO USE:
- Styrofoam or paper cup
- Styrofoam ball
- plastic drinking straw
- felt tip pens
- felt, fabric, yarn and/or ribbon scraps
- scissors

## WHAT TO DO:
1. Decide who you want your pop-up puppet to be.
2. Use the felt tip pens to draw facial features on the Styrofoam ball.
3. Make a hat, hair or other decorative trim from the fabric scraps.
4. Use the scissors to poke a hole for the straw in the bottom of the ball.
5. Stick the straw into the hole in the head.
6. Make a hole in the bottom of the cup and push the bottom of the straw through it.
7. Your pop-up puppet will be ready to pop in and out of its hiding place whenever you push the straw.

# GYPSY ROSE RISES AGAIN

*she has personality plus — a pencil*

**WHAT TO USE:**
- pencil
- tissues
- bandana
- black yarn
- beaded necklace or bracelet
- construction paper
- scissors
- felt tip pens
- glue

**WHAT TO DO:**
1. Wrap a bunch of tissues around the top of the pencil.
2. Drape the bandana over the top of the pencil and tie it tightly with a piece of yarn to form a neck.
3. Use a piece of white construction paper and felt tip pens to draw a face. Glue the face on.
4. Make lots of wild, black hair from the yarn and glue in place.
5. Make construction paper earrings or other decorations and glue these on too.
6. If you have an old beaded necklace or bracelet, drape that over the gypsy's head.

# A ROYAL COURT

*fit for a king and queen*

**WHAT TO USE:**
- Styrofoam ball or tennis ball
- knife
- felt tip pens
- white handkerchief
- construction paper
- glue
- scissors

**WHAT TO DO:**
1. Cut a hole a little larger than your second finger on one side of the ball. (Ask for help if you need it.)
2. Make facial features with construction paper or with felt tip pens.
3. Make a crown from construction paper and glue it on.

4. Use the felt tip pens to draw a royal costume for the king on the handkerchief.
5. Drape the handkerchief over your hand and push your finger into the hole in the ball.
6. Extend your thumb and little finger for the puppet's arms.

# MARIONETTE MAGIC

*with the pull of a string, they can dance and sing*

This is a simple marionette that can be made without lots of extra materials. More complicated marionettes can be constructed with wood which allows more movement. Many import stores carry marionettes that can be purchased inexpensively and dressed up with clothes and other odds and ends.

**WHAT TO USE:**
- stiff paper
- pencil
- scissors
- hole punch
- 2 brads
- string

**WHAT TO DO:**

1. Draw a character you like on the piece of paper. Draw the arms separately (see illustration).
2. Punch holes at the character's head, tops of the arms and bottom of the hands with the hole punch.

punch
holes

3. Attach the arms with the brads.
4. Tie a piece of string onto each hole.
5. Make a slip knot at the other end of the string.
6. Place the hand strings on your thumb and little finger and the head string around your index finger. These will operate your marionette.

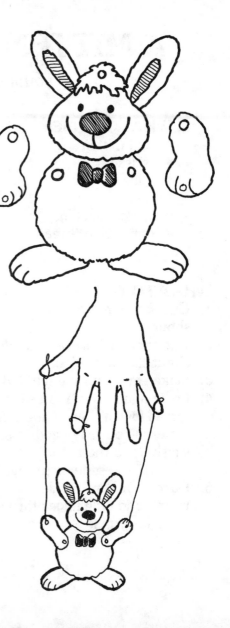

# A MITTEN OR A KITTEN?

*you just need to meow*

**WHAT TO USE:**
- old mitten
- scissors
- glue
- felt
- yellow sequins
- stiff nylon thread

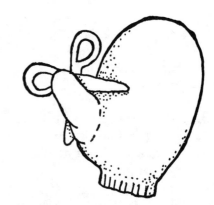

**WHAT TO DO:**
1. Cut the thumb off the mitten as shown.
2. Cut another hole on the other side about the same size.
3. Make ears from the felt and glue on.
4. Make a felt nose and use the nylon thread for whiskers. Glue that on the mitten. (You may need to sew the whiskers to the felt.)
5. Glue on the sequins for eyes.
6. Place your hand inside and put your thumb and little finger through the holes for arms.

# THUMB ALONG

*singing a song*

## WHAT TO USE:
- your very own thumb
- washable pens

## WHAT TO DO:
1. Draw a singing face on your very clean thumb.
2. Do the same thing on your other thumb for a duet!

# FANCY FLORA AND FADED FRED

*could these two want to wed?*

**WHAT TO USE:**
- nylon stockings
- ribbon
- felt tip pens
- earrings
- yarn
- glue

**WHAT TO DO:**
1. Cut one nylon stocking so that it reaches your forearm when you put your hand inside.
2. Stuff a bunch of other stockings in the toe. This will be the puppet's head.
3. For Flora, cut strips of stockings and tie ribbons on the ends and glue them on for hair. Draw on a heart-shaped mouth, big eyes, long, long eyelashes and red cheeks. Find some old pierced earrings to stick into the stocking.

4. For Fred, use yarn for hair, and draw on a sad, sad face with the felt tip pens. Give him some freckles too for fun.

5. Wiggle your hand in between the stockings to operate these two characters.

You may kiss the bride

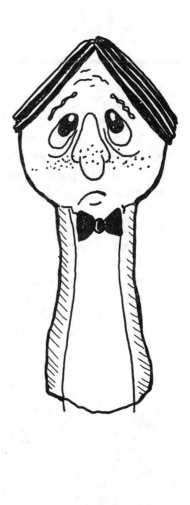

# ISN'T IT AMAZING WHAT A HAND CAN DO?

*— especially if it's on you!*

**WHAT TO USE:**
- washable felt tip pens
- lipstick, rouge, eye shadow (if you have it)
- scarf or handkerchief
- scraps of paper, cloth, yarn or ribbon
- and your hand, of course

**WHAT TO DO:**
1. Spread your amazing hand out in front of you. Think of all the things you can make it do — wiggle your fingers; snap, stretch, point, twist and intertwine them; crook the thumb; make a fist; wave and send signals.

2. Now your hand should be limbered up and ready to become a puppet extraordinaire! Place it like this.

3. Then, move your thumb around to make the movement of a mouth opening and closing, smiling, frowning, coughing, hiccuping, laughing, pouting, singing, shouting and on and on.

4. Next, wiggle your whole hand while making the mouth work. As you experiment, you will decide on the puppet character you want to turn your amazing hand into.

5. Use the pens and/or makeup to draw eyes, nose, lips, beard, mustache, freckles, etc. on your hand.

6. Use the scarf, scraps or whatever you have handy for finishing touches. Try some of these if you like, or just let your imagination take over for even more fanciful figures.

# TEN LITTLE GLOVE FINGERS

*make ten little Indians*

**WHAT TO USE:**
- old glove
- scissors
- colored felt pieces
- sequins, small buttons, yarn
- needle and thread

**WHAT TO DO:**
1. Cut the fingers off an old glove.
2. Decorate the Indians by adding a feather headband made from felt, war paint on cheeks, sequin eyes and yarn for hair. Sew the decorations in place.
3. Gather them together for a powwow, rain dance or whatever you want them to do. Ten little Indians can go a long way!

# FEET FIRST

*for a first-rate audience*

## WHAT TO USE:
- a pair of footies
- scissors
- needle and thread or glue
- fabric or felt
- yarn or other trim
- mirror

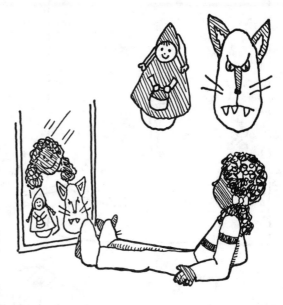

## WHAT TO DO:
1. Put the footies on your feet.
2. Stretch out on the floor so that you can see the bottoms of your feet in the mirror.
3. Decide what kind of puppet characters you want to turn your feet into.
4. Take the footies off your feet and plan the facial features and trim for your two "feet first" puppets.
5. Remember, you will always be playing to a very important audience (you), so choose interesting characters (Flopsy and Mopsy Cottontail, Little Red Riding Hood and the Wolf, The Hare and the Tortoise, etc.).
6. Stretch your puppets out in front of the mirror and let the show begin.

# RABBIT RALLY

*for a jumping good time*

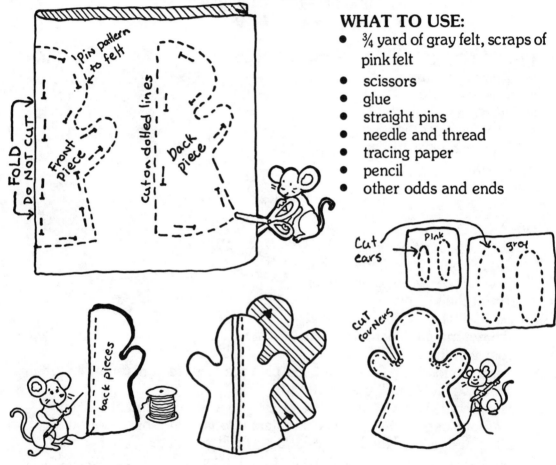

**WHAT TO USE:**

- ¾ yard of gray felt, scraps of pink felt
- scissors
- glue
- straight pins
- needle and thread
- tracing paper
- pencil
- other odds and ends

Pin pattern to felt

FOLD — Do Not Cut

Front Piece

Cut on dotted lines

Back Piece

Cut ears — Pink — gray

back pieces

Cut corners

**WHAT TO DO:**

1. Cut the ¾ yard of felt to a ½ yard piece.
2. Fold the felt in half as shown.
3. Draw shapes similar to the ones shown on a piece of tracing paper and cut them out.
4. Place the front piece along the folded side of the felt and pin in place.
5. Pin the back piece alongside the front piece (not on a fold).
6. Carefully cut the pieces out (do not cut along the fold). You should have two back pieces and one front piece.
7. Pin the right sides of the two back pieces together and sew together as shown.
8. Place the right sides of the front and back together and stitch around the entire puppet.
9. Turn the puppet inside out and press with medium-hot iron.
10. You may want to hem the bottom of the puppet. If so, turn the felt ¼ inch to the inside and stitch.
11. Cut out ears as shown from gray felt. Add the inside pink pieces and glue on.
12. You can add your own ideas for paws, whiskers, eyes, nose and mouth.
13. Stick your hand inside and your rabbit will be ready to hop!

# AN OLD SWEATER NEVER HAD IT BETTER

*turn one into a puppet!*

Save your old sweaters! You can save the buttons for eyes, nose, earrings; use the button holes for finger spaces or to run yarn hair through and the ribbing can be used for trim, etc.

The sleeves can be used for long animal puppets and the front and back for cloth-type puppets. If you don't have a sweater, don't despair — use an old pajama top or shirt; but a sweater is really better because it stretches to fit your needs.

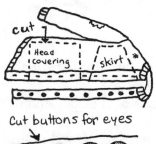

cut

Head covering

skirt

Cut buttons for eyes

Styrofoam ball

tie cloth around stick with yarn or ribbing

string yarn through holes

string ribbon through holes

# SEE YOU LATER, ALLIGATOR

*after while, crocodile*

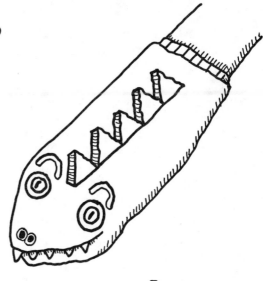

**WHAT TO USE:**
- old sweater sleeve
- needle and thread
- buttons
- white and green felt
- glue
- scissors

**WHAT TO DO:**
1. Cut off the sweater sleeve at the elbow.
2. Sew one end together to use for the alligator's head. Leave the other end open to insert your hand and arm.
3. Glue on white teeth and green scales.
4. Sew on buttons for eyes.

# MORE ABOUT PUPPETS

# MATERIALS TO COLLECT

**For hair** — knitting yarn, crochet thread, rug wool, scraps of fur, macramé cord, pieces of rope, unraveled pot scrubbers, strips of old nylon hose, string, gift wrap ties, felt strips, straw, etc.

**For facial features** — buttons, beads, scraps of fancy paper, felt tip pens, pasta (with holes), old makeup, felt scraps, etc.

**For costumes** — silk scarves, handkerchiefs, pieces of fabric such as silk, cotton, flannel, wool plaid, velvet, tissue or crepe paper, bandanas, etc.

# AND SAVE FOR PUPPET MAKING

**For decoration** — beads, old jewelry (pins, gold chains, rings, earrings), small silk flowers, gold and silver braid, fancy rickrack, sequins, feathers, etc.

**For heads** — tennis balls, Styrofoam balls, papier mâché, waded up tissues.

**For hands** — felt scraps, cotton (for stuffing), gloves.

# PUT YOUR PUPPETS ON STAGE

*and your play will be all the rage*

Here are some ideas for stages. Try a few of these or think up some of your own!

JOY'S PUPPET SHOW

Find a big box & you can get inside

shoe box for finger puppets

THE PALM CIRCLE PUPPET PEOPLE

Tape a big piece of cardboard to a table for your own 3-ring circus

You can use an old sheet with an opening cut in it- you can decorate it too

Cut open a cardboard box
& make a scene

Turn a chalk board
into a puppet stage

Open a downstairs window—
you can perform indoors or out

Attach a
rocker to
a boat-shaped
piece of
cardboard
& take your
puppets
to sea

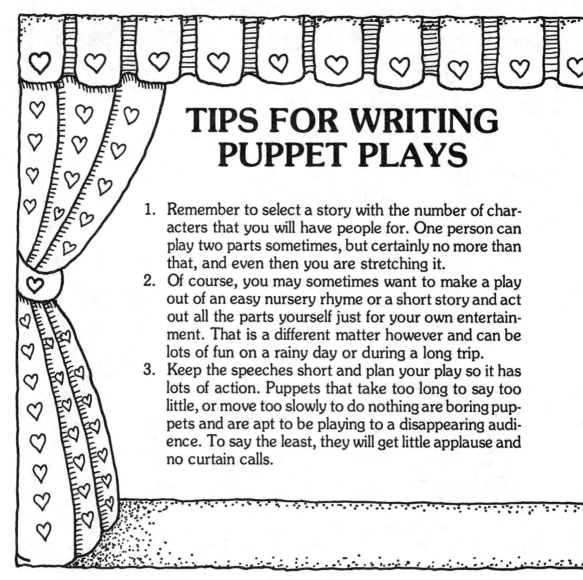

# TIPS FOR WRITING PUPPET PLAYS

1. Remember to select a story with the number of characters that you will have people for. One person can play two parts sometimes, but certainly no more than that, and even then you are stretching it.
2. Of course, you may sometimes want to make a play out of an easy nursery rhyme or a short story and act out all the parts yourself just for your own entertainment. That is a different matter however and can be lots of fun on a rainy day or during a long trip.
3. Keep the speeches short and plan your play so it has lots of action. Puppets that take too long to say too little, or move too slowly to do nothing are boring puppets and are apt to be playing to a disappearing audience. To say the least, they will get little applause and no curtain calls.

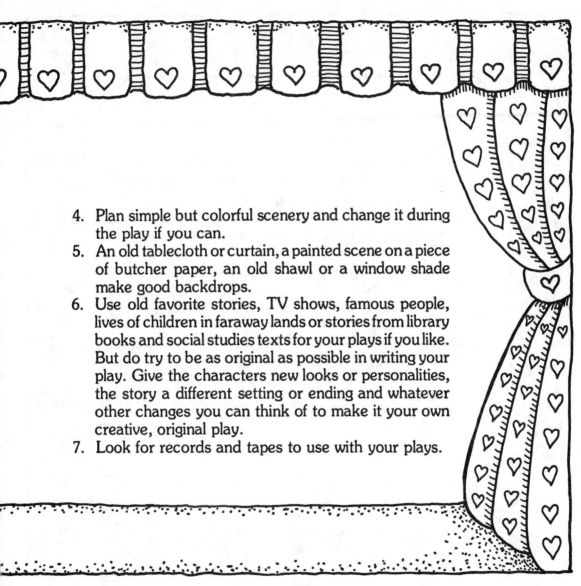

4. Plan simple but colorful scenery and change it during the play if you can.
5. An old tablecloth or curtain, a painted scene on a piece of butcher paper, an old shawl or a window shade make good backdrops.
6. Use old favorite stories, TV shows, famous people, lives of children in faraway lands or stories from library books and social studies texts for your plays if you like. But do try to be as original as possible in writing your play. Give the characters new looks or personalities, the story a different setting or ending and whatever other changes you can think of to make it your own creative, original play.
7. Look for records and tapes to use with your plays.

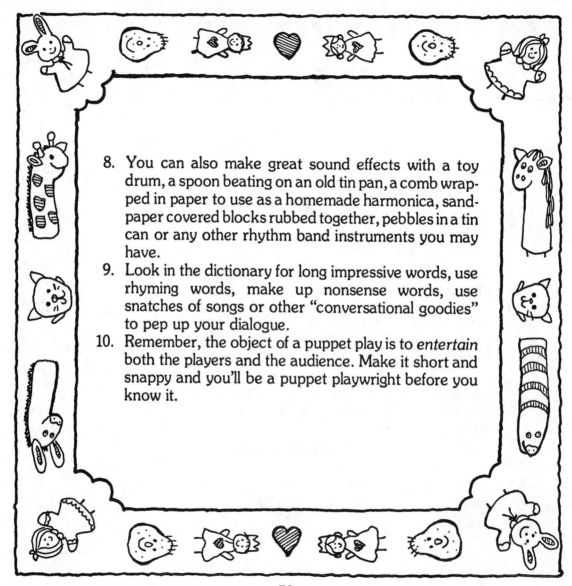

8. You can also make great sound effects with a toy drum, a spoon beating on an old tin pan, a comb wrapped in paper to use as a homemade harmonica, sandpaper covered blocks rubbed together, pebbles in a tin can or any other rhythm band instruments you may have.

9. Look in the dictionary for long impressive words, use rhyming words, make up nonsense words, use snatches of songs or other "conversational goodies" to pep up your dialogue.

10. Remember, the object of a puppet play is to *entertain* both the players and the audience. Make it short and snappy and you'll be a puppet playwright before you know it.

# AND THEY LIVED HAPPILY EVER AFTER

## *or did they?*

Select your favorite fairy tale to make into a puppet play. Make rod puppets to act out your play. To make a rod puppet, you simply draw the figure on heavy paper (such as construction paper or tagboard), cut it out and attach it to a stick.

You can paste on bits of cotton, braid, old jewelry or other odds and ends to add interest to the figures if you like.

Your puppet plays can be made more interesting by changing the familiar setting to a modern one by switching the characters' personalities around, by changing the plot and sequence of events or by giving the play a surprise ending. For example, you might do Cinderella with a space-age theme, making the step sisters good-hearted, and the stepmother sick in bed, the pumpkin a spaceship and the prince a visitor from another planet. Now, that would be a switch wouldn't it?

tape puppet to stick

73

# FAIRY TALES FOR PUPPETS TO ACT OUT

| Fairy Tale | Puppet Characters/Props |
|---|---|
| Rumpelstiltskin | poor miller, beautiful daughter, mayor, king, Rumpelstiltskin, baby, messenger |
| Goldilocks & the Three Bears | Goldilocks, father bear, mother bear, baby bear |
| Little Red Riding Hood | Little Red Riding Hood, woodcutter, wolf, grandmother |

| | |
|---|---|
| Snow White & the Seven Dwarfs | queen, Snow White, huntsman, dwarves, prince, mirror |
| The Elves & the Shoemaker | shoemaker, wife, customers, elves |
| Jack & the Beanstalk | mother, Jack, man, giant, wife |
| Little Red Hen | Little Red Hen, pig, duck, cat |
| Three Little Pigs | Three Little Pigs, wolf |
| Three Billy Goats Gruff | big billy goat, middle-sized billy goat, little billy goat, troll |

# ONE PERSON DOES THE TALKING

*the others do the acting*

One good way to stage a puppet play is for a narrator to read all the parts of the entire story while other actors perform. This is an especially good way to do a play with rhyming words or word patterns or one with difficult to remember speaking parts.

Suggestions for stories to do with a narrator include:

The Hare and the Tortoise
Noah's Ark
The life of a famous person
The Night Before Christmas
Dr. Seuss stories such as
    Horton Hatches an Egg
Aesop's Fables
The Little Red Hen
The Three Bears
Hans Christian Anderson's
    The Ugly Duckling
The Emperor's New Clothes
Maurice Sendak's
    Where the Wild Things Are
Ezra Jack Keat's Snowy Day

# INDEX

**A**

Alligator puppet, 63

**B**

Ball puppet, 48-49
Balloons
    for heads, 26-28
    bogeymen, 44
Balls
    for heads, 26-28, 46, 48-49
Bandana, 47
Bathtub
    friend, 29
Beans, 42-43
Bowl, 40-41
Box puppet, 35
Broom puppet, 33

**C**

Can
    juice, 42-43
Cardboard roll, 16
Catalogs, 21
Cereal box puppet, 35
Cereal
    dry, 42-43
Clay
    for heads, 26-28
Cloth puppet, 60-61, 62
Clothespin puppet, 30
Construction paper puppet, 20
Costumes, 66-67
Cowboys, 30
Cup, 40-41, 46

**D**

Decorations, 66-67

**E**

Eggshells, 26-28
Elves, 22-23
Elves and the Shoemaker, 74-75

**F**

Fabric puppet, 60-61, 62
Facial features, 66-67
Fairy tales, 73, 74-75
Feet, 59
Finger puppets, 12-13, 16, 21, 22-23,
    24, 44, 58
Flashlight, 14-15
Flowers, 18-19
Forks
    as puppets, 40-41

**G**

Gingerbread Man, 14-15
Glove, 58
Goldilocks, 74-75
Gypsy, 47

**H**

Hair, 66-67
Hairbrush, 32
Hand puppet, 56-57
Hand towel, 29
Handkerchief, 48-49, 56-57
Hands, 66-67
Heads
    for puppets, 26-28, 66-67
Holiday puppet, 22-23
Hose puppet, 54-55

**I**

Indians, 58

**J**

Jack and the Beanstalk, 74-75
Jewelry, 47, 54-55
Juice can puppet, 42-43

**K**

King puppet, 48-49
Kitten puppet, 52
Knives
    as puppets, 40-41

**L**
Lad, 12-13
Lassie, 12-13
Leaves, 18
Leprechaun, 12-13
Life-size puppet, 33
Little Red Hen, 74-75
Little Red Riding Hood, 74-75
Lizard puppet, 20

**M**
Magazines, 21
Makeup, 56-57
Marionette, 50-51
Mitten puppet, 52
Mirror, 59
Monster puppet, 42-43
Musician, 16

**N**
Narrator, 76-77
Newspaper
    for heads, 26-28
Nuts, 34, 38, 39

**P**
Paints, 33
Pancake turner puppet, 34
Paper bag puppet, 17, 42-43
Paper bowls, 40-41
Paper cups, 40-41, 46
Paper plate puppet, 18-19
Papier mâché heads, 26-28
Pasta, 34, 38, 39, 42-43
Pencil puppet, 31, 47
Picnic, 40-41
Pillowcase, 33
Plastic tableware, 40-41
Play dough
    for heads, 26-28
Plays, 70-72, 73, 76-77
Pop-up puppet, 46
Potato puppet, 38

**Q**
Queen puppet, 48-49

**R**
Rabbit puppet, 60-61
Reptiles, 20, 36-37, 63
Rice, 34, 39, 43-43
Rumpelstiltskin, 74-75

**S**
Santa Claus, 22-23
Sewing, 29, 36-37, 58, 59, 60-61, 63
Shadow puppet, 14-15
Shapes, 25
Snake puppet, 36-37
Snow White, 74-75
Soap opera, 21
Sock puppet, 36-37
Spaceman, 31
Sponge puppet, 31
Spoons
    as puppets, 40-41
Spud puppet, 38
Stages, 68-69
Sticks, 25, 39, 42-43
Stocking puppet, 54-55
Straw puppet, 14-15, 46
Sweater puppet, 62-63

**T**
Thumb puppet, 53
Three Billy Goats Gruff, 74-75
Three Little Pigs, 74-75

**W**
Walking puppet, 24
Walnut puppet, 39
Walrus puppet, 17
Washcloth, 29
Wood scrap puppet, 45